Get a Grip!

by Melissa Stewart

P9-AGD-491

Welcome to the lab! To assemble and start using your skeletal hand right away, turn to page 24!

Get a Grip!

Copyright becker&mayer!, 11010 Northup Way, Bellevue, Washington. Published 2005.

Published by SmartLab®, an imprint of becker&mayer!
All rights reserved. SmartLab® is a registered trademark of becker&mayer!, 11010 Northup Way, Bellevue, Washington.
Creative development by Jim Becker and Anna Johnson

If you have questions or comments about this product, send e-mail to info@smartlabtoys.com or visit www.smartlabtoys.com.

Edited by Ben Grossblatt
Written by Melissa Stewart
Designed by Lisa M. Douglass
Illustrations and package design by Eddee Helms
Assembly illustrations by Ryan Hobson
Medical illustrations by Jennifer Fairman
X-ray illustrations by Kristen Weinandt Marzejon
Product photography by Keith Megay
SmartLab® character photography by Craig Harrold
Product development by Mark Byrnes
Production management by Katie Stephens
Project management by Beth Lenz

Printed, manufactured, and assembled in China.

Get a Grip! is part of the SmartLab® You Control It Skeletal Hand kit. Not to be sold separately.

10 9 8 7 6 5 4 3 2
1-932855-26-2
05255

YOUR HELPING HANDS

Your hand weighs less than 1 pound, but it's one of the most important parts of your body. Think of all the ways you use your hands every day.

Without hands, you couldn't hold your toothbrush or squeeze a tube of toothpaste. You couldn't comb your hair or button a shirt. You couldn't lift a fork or drink a glass of juice.

You'd have trouble climbing aboard the school bus, and just imagine trying to scratch an itchy nose. You couldn't give your friend a thumbs-up or hold a sandwich in the cafeteria. And how would you write, type, or draw with no hands? A life without hands would be pretty tough.

THE HUMAN HAND CAN GRIP AND HOLD THINGS IN THREE DIFFERENT WAYS.

POWER GRIP

You rest an object in the palm of your hand and wrap your fingers around it. This is how you hold a screwdriver or a tennis racket.

PRECISION GRIP

You hold an object between the tips of your thumb and index finger. This is how you pick up small objects, such as an earring or a quarter.

HOOK GRIP

You hook your fingers around an object and pull it toward you. This is how you open a door or pick up a drinking glass.

THE NAME GAME

When scientists and doctors talk about a person's fingers, they use numbers—1, 2, 3, 4, and 5. But most people use the names thumb, pointer finger (or index finger), middle finger, ring finger, and little finger (or pinkie).

WHO HAS HANDS?

handy, but not a hand.

Do dogs and cats? How about rabbits and monkeys? Do these sound like totally easy questions? Maybe they're not, after all. Let's take a look.

According to scientists, a hand consists of a broad palm with four fingers and a thumb. A thumb is very special because it is *opposable*. It's set opposite your four fingers and can swivel to touch them. This allows you to hold things.

Dogs and cats don't have opposable thumbs, but other animals do. Humans are members of an animal group called the primates. From fist-sized galagos to 400-pound gorillas, all primates have arms and legs that can move freely, as well as flexible fingers and toes. They also have large brains and forward-facing eyes that can judge distances accurately.

More space in your brain is devoted to controlling your thumbs than any other body part. Thumbs are that important!

THUMBS UP!

FORWARD FACING EYES

BIG BRAIN

FLEXIBLE FINGERS

FREELY MOVING ARMS

The first primates lived on Earth about 65 million years ago. As time passed, many new groups of primates evolved. One of these groups was the monkeys that now live in the tropical forests of Central and South America. A second group of monkeys developed in Africa.

About 23 million years ago, a few African monkeys evolved into a group called the hominoids. As more time passed, early hominoids developed into the great apes—orangutans, gorillas, bonobos, and chimpanzees—and then into humans. Like people, great apes are active during the day and sleep at night. They have excellent eyesight and see the world in a full range of vivid colors. Most importantly, all great apes have opposable thumbs. So do some monkeys.

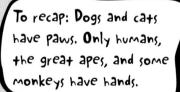

To recap: Dogs and cats have paws. Only humans, the great apes, and some monkeys have hands.

UNDERNEATH IT ALL

If you could peel back the skin on your hand, you'd see muscles and nerves and blood vessels. But underneath it all are twenty-seven bones. They give your hand its shape and strength.

CARPALS

The eight small, cube-shaped bones in your wrist are arranged in two rows of four. They allow you to bend and twist your hand in any direction.

METACARPALS

These five long, thin bones span your palm. Metacarpals let you make a fist.

PHALANGES

Each finger has three segments or phalanges (fuh-LAN-jeez). Your thumb has two. That adds up to 14 phalanges on each hand. The place where two phalanges meet is called a knuckle. This is where your fingers bend.

STARE AND COMPARE

Even though other animals don't have hands, it's interesting to compare the bones in their limbs to ours. All the animals below have the same basic bones. This shows that we are distantly related to birds, bats, and alligators.

A **human** has long arms that bend at the elbow and hands with opposable thumbs. That's why we can grasp and hold objects.

A **bat's** long metacarpals and phalanges support the thin skin that stretches over them. Even though a bat's wings are very different from a bird's wings, both structures accomplish the same goal—they make flight possible.

A **bird's** bones are shorter and smaller. Some are fused together. This makes the bird's wings lightweight, so it can fly.

Compared to its size, an **alligator** has arm bones about the same size as a bird's, but they are positioned more like a human's. The carpals are large. The metacarpals and phalanges spread widely. The alligator's strong carpals support its weight as it walks on land. Webbing between phalanges helps an alligator swim.

The shape and position of the bones in each animal's front limbs are different. Over millions of years, the animals' bodies have undergone changes, so they are perfectly adapted to survive in their environments.

HANDS  ON THE MOVE

How many ways can you move your hands? You can push and pull, grab and hold, pinch and poke, squeeze and signal. Muscles control all these motions. Your hand has about thirty muscles. They are divided into five main groups.

MIDPALMERS

These muscles are located in the palm of your hand. They bend and straighten the joints between your phalanges and metacarpals.

THENARS

These muscles run along the outside of your thumb. They allow your thumb to grasp objects.

FLEXORS

These muscles are located on the underside of your forearm. Long strips of tissue called tendons attach them to your phalanges. They allow you to bend your fingers and thumb.

EXTENSORS

These muscles are located on the back of your forearm. Long strips of tissue called tendons attach them to your phalanges. They allow you to straighten your fingers and thumb.

HYPNOTHENARS

These muscles run along the outside of your pinkie. They make it possible for you to stick your pinkie out straight while making a fist. (Just try to do this with your ring finger!)

Want stronger hands? Here are some ways to exercise your hand muscles.

STRONGER HANDS

Hold your arm out straight, fingers pointing up and palm open (the "Stop in the name of the law!" pose). Gently pull your fingers back toward you with your other hand. Hold them that way for 10 seconds. Repeat several times with each hand.

Place a rubber ball in your palm and squeeze it as hard as you can for one second. Open your hand. Repeat 30 times with each hand.

YOU'VE GOT NERVE

How do your hand muscles know when to flex and when to relax? They follow directions from your brain. When you want to operate your TV remote control, your brain sends a message to the muscles that move your thumb. When you want do something more complicated, like peel an orange, dozens of messages whiz through your nerve cells. Each message controls a specific part of the job. Some of the nerves in your hand don't have anything to do with controlling muscles. Sensors at the tips of these nerves are specially designed to detect pressure, pain, heat, and cold.

HANDY EXPERIMENT

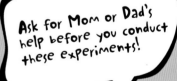

Ask for Mom or Dad's help before you conduct these experiments!

To start your experiment, first find a paperclip. Straighten out one end of it. With a washable marker, draw a box the size of a postage stamp on the back of your hand. Divide the box into sixteen smaller squares by drawing three lines across and three lines up and down. Draw a larger copy of the box on a piece of paper.

PRESSURE SENSORS

To find pressure sensors in the skin of your hand, touch the curved part of the paperclip to the squares on the back of your hand. If you can feel the paperclip pressing your skin, write a P in the same box in the bigger square you drew.

COLD SENSORS

To find cold sensors, hold one end of the paperclip against an ice cube. Touch the chilled paperclip to one of the squares on your hand. If you feel it, write a C in the corresponding section of the paper. Cool the paperclip again before testing the next square.

HEAT SENSORS

To find heat sensors, dip the end of the paperclip into hot water and count to ten. (Get a parent's help for this part—you don't want the paperclip to be too hot!) Then touch one of the squares on your hand. Can you feel it? If so, write an H in the corresponding section of the paper. Be sure to re-heat the paperclip between each test.

PAIN SENSORS

To find pain sensors... Well, we don't need to go looking for pain sensors now, do we? We know they're there!

LOOK AT THE PIECE OF PAPER WHEN YOU'VE FINISHED ALL YOUR TESTS.

ARE YOU SURPRISED BY YOUR RESULTS?

COLD HANDS, WARM HEART

Imagine it: You don't feel cold, but your hands are freezing and your fingernails are turning blue. What's going on here?

When your body is fighting to stay warm, your body focuses on heating your most important organs, like your brain and heart.

To get more blood pumping to your hands . . .

- **PUT ON A SWEATER (YOUR COLD VITAL ORGANS WON'T NEED AS MUCH BLOOD PUMPED TO THEM).**
- **EXERCISE.**
- **HAVE SOME HOT SOUP OR COCOA.**

FINGERNAILS?

When you look at your hands, what's the first thing you notice? Probably your skin. But take a closer look. What do you see? At the tip of each finger is a hard, sharp fingernail.

KERATIN

Fingernails are made of a protein called keratin (CARE-uh-tin). Like your hair, your fingernails are made of dead cells. They grow out of the skin at the base of the nail.

Claws are made out of the same stuff as fingernails!

NO BITING!

CUTICLE

BASE

STRENGTH

Fingernails protect your fingertips, and they add strength and stiffness to your uppermost phalanges. They help you pick up small objects, like coins, and nothing's better at relieving an annoying itch.

GROWTH

Fingernails grow about one inch every eight months, but some nails grow faster than others. The nail on your middle finger grows the fastest. The nails on your thumb and pinky grow the slowest. Fingernails grow more quickly during the day and in the summer. They grow faster in children than in adults. If you're right-handed, the nails on that hand grow more rapidly. If you're left-handed, your left hand's nails grow faster.

Dogs can be right-handed or left-handed too!

RIGHT HAND OR LEFT HAND

About one in ten people is left-handed. Nobody knows why these people prefer to use their left hands for writing, reaching, and other tasks. What we do know is that being a lefty is nothing new.

Between 10 and 20 percent of the hand tracings left on cave walls by Cro-Magnon people were right hands, showing that even 14,000 years ago some people were left handed. (Those left-handed people must have preferred tracing their *right* hands with their *left* hands.) Lefties are just as capable as righties. But being left-handed in a right-handed world can be difficult.

Lefties often have to use right-handed scissors, cameras, can openers, and spiral notebooks. While eating, lefties often bump elbows with their right-handed table neighbors. Lefties may have trouble learning how to knit or tie a shoe if they are taught by a right-handed person.

HOW ABOUT A
KNUCKLE SANDWICH?

Our hands are creased with dozens of lines. The most prominent lines on your fingers mark your knuckles. A knuckle is a joint—the area where two bones come together—between two phalanges or between a phalange and a metacarpal. A liquid called synovial (suh-NO-vee-ul) fluid fills the space between the bones.

KNUCKLE

Do you like to "crack" your knuckles? As you pull on a joint, the pressure inside drops. Your ligaments get sucked in. When the pressure is low enough, tiny bubbles form in the synovial fluid. The popping noise you may hear comes from vibrations caused by the breaking bubbles or by the ligaments snapping back into place. Knuckle cracking doesn't cause arthritis, but it can lead to some weakness in your hand.

Have you ever seen someone who can bend their thumb in strange ways? People say they are double-jointed, but they don't really have two joints. Instead, their joints are extra flexible. This could be because the bone ends are smoother than normal or because the ligaments—bands of tissue that stretch across joints—are extra stretchy.

SOME HANDY
EXPRESSIONS

WANT A KNUCKLE SANDWICH?

This is the way hand fans intimidate people. It's another way of saying, "How'd like you a punch in the mouth?"

(Note: There is no way to ask this question politely.)

HAND-ME-DOWN

Clothes, toys, or other old junk passed from an older child to a younger one.

(Note: Parents love hand-me-downs. No one else does.)

SHE KNOWS IT LIKE THE BACK OF HER HAND

It's as familiar to her as the back of her hand is. She knows something very well, as if she were born with the knowledge.

(Note: Wait, was that birthmark always there?)

RIGHT-HAND MAN

If someone is your right-hand man, he's as important to you as your right hand. In other words, he helps you pull on your socks and open bottles of soda.

(Note: Lefties may substitute "left" every place "right" appears above.)

GIVE HER A HAND

Help her out, or give her a round of applause.

(Note: When someone kicks over a ladder, ends up clinging to the chandelier, and asks, "Can you give me a hand?" she's not asking for you to clap.)

Some people claim they can predict the future by "reading" the lines on another person's palm. Me, I'm skeptical.

ON THE TIPS OF YOUR FINGERS

Look closely at your fingertips. You should see tiny ridges on your skin. These ridges help you get a grip on things. Like the treads on a tire, the ridges on your fingers grab a surface and prevent slipping and skidding.

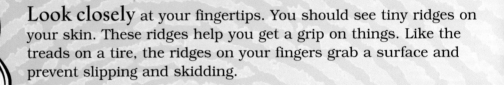

1 Place a sheet of paper on a flat table. Press firmly on one end of the paper with the fingers on your right hand. Press lightly on the other end with the fingers on your left hand. Using your left hand, push gently on the paper and watch it rise up in the middle.

2 Now try to gently push on the paper with your wrist or the back of your hand. The experiment won't work with other body parts because only your fingers have ridges.

HANDY EXPERIMENT

RIDGES

LOOP

WHORL

ARCH

The ridges on your fingertips are arranged in patterns made up of loops, whorls, and arches. When you touch something, you often leave behind a mark with that pattern of ridges. It's your fingerprint. Each person's fingerprints are a unique design of ridges, so they are an excellent way to identify people. Police officers often use fingerprints to identify missing persons and criminals.

About two-thirds of all people have looped fingerprints. Some people have two loops that curl around each other. About one-third of people have whorls. These fingerprints have a full circle at the center. Only a small number of people have arched fingerprints.

FINGERPRINTS

To see which kind of fingerprints you have, cover a large area of a white piece of paper with dark pencil marks. Rub the tip of one finger on the pencil marks. To "lift" the print, place a piece of transparent tape across your fingertip. Gently remove the tape from your finger and transfer the print to another white piece of paper. Repeat this process for each of your fingers. Then compare your fingerprints to the pictures on the left.

Criminals have tried scrubbing their fingertips with sandpaper, burning them with acid, and peeling the skin away, all to keep from being identified and caught by police. But when all these wounds healed and new skin grew back, the same patterns reappeared.

YOUR HANDS SAY SO

HANDY EXPERIMENT

Have you ever waved hello to someone? Have you given your friends a thumbs-up to let them know everything is okay? Maybe you've held up your hand to tell someone to stop. Each time, you were using your hands to communicate.

Most of the time, people communicate by talking, but hands can be really important for getting a message across. How many different hand signals can you think of?

If a person's hands are open with the palms up, they feel friendly and are probably telling the truth.

If someone hides their hands or has their palms down, they might feel angry or worried. They might also be hiding the truth.

It should be no surprise that a clenched fist spells trouble.

LET YOUR FINGERS DO THE TALKING

Of course, we also use our hands to write and draw. These are two very important forms of communication. Deaf people often use a sign language—a complex language of hand movements. People who are fluent in a sign language can "talk" as quickly as people using spoken words.

FROG

A. Make a fist under your chin.

B. Flick your index and middle finger outward.

SCIENCE

Pretend to pour something from two beakers.

Long ago, many different Native American tribes lived on the Great Plains of North America. Each tribe spoke a slightly different language. When people from different tribes met, they used a common set of hand signs to communicate.

"dog"

WHEN HANDS HURT

Most of us take our hands for granted—until they get hurt. Luckily, most hand injuries are minor. Cuts, scrapes, slivers, and minor burns usually heal in about week. Even a broken finger isn't such a big deal. After wearing a splint for a few weeks, the finger is as good as new.

HAVS

Some hand injuries can be more serious. Do your hands ever get tired and stiff when you play video games? A 15-year-old boy in England used his videogame console so much that he developed an unusual medical condition. In cold weather, the boy's fingers turned white and became swollen. In warm weather, his fingers turned red and hurt.

At first doctors weren't sure what was going on. But eventually, they diagnosed him with hand-arm vibration syndrome (HAVS). This condition usually affects people who spend a lot of time operating jackhammers or chainsaws. According to doctors, the boy developed HAVS from playing video games for up to seven hours at a time. Playing video games can also cause central palmar blisters. These painful blisters can develop when a person's palms rub against a joystick for long periods of time.

CARPAL TUNNEL SYNDROME

Another problem that can develop in the hands is carpal tunnel syndrome. The name refers to a tunnel, or tube, between the wrist bones. A nerve and the tendons that control the fingers pass through this tube. If you perform certain activities over and over, for a long time, the tendons can swell up and pinch the nerve. The result can be numbness in the hand or tingling, pain, or weakness.

CARPAL TUNNEL

MOVEMENTS THAT MIGHT LEAD TO CARPAL TUNNEL SYNDROME

- TYPING
- USING TOOLS LIKE SHOVELS AND POWER TOOLS THAT VIBRATE
- GRIPPING STEERING WHEELS TIGHTLY
- PLAYING MUSICAL INSTRUMENTS

A HANDY HOBBY

Dr. Adrian Flatt, a retired hand surgeon, has an unusual hobby. For the last 40 years, he's been making bronze casts of people's hands. His collection, which is now on display at Baylor University Medical Center in Dallas, Texas, includes samples from dozens of doctors, seven presidents, ten astronauts, and ten entertainers. Among the people whose hands have been immortalized in bronze are Walt Disney, basketball great Wilt Chamberlain, legendary news anchorman Walter Cronkite, magician David Copperfield, musician Louis Armstrong, and wrestler Andre the Giant.

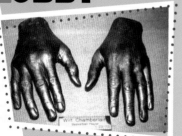

Wilt Chamberlain

What? No paws?!

23

ASSEMBLY
INSTRUCTIONS

FINGERPADS

THUMB

GRIP

HAND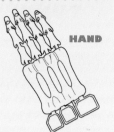

STEP 1

Attach the grip to the hand by inserting the three pegs on the grip into the holes in the palm-side of the wrist. When the pegs are in all the way, you'll hear a click.

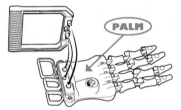

PALM

STEP 2

Insert the four-part thumb peg into the socket. Make sure the small pin beside the thumb peg fits into the wider slot in the socket.

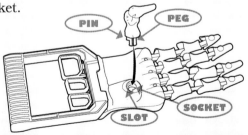

PIN PEG SLOT SOCKET

STEP 3

Peel a fingerpad from the backing and press it into the circular indentation in a fingertip. Repeat this, one fingerpad at a time, with the other three pads. Only the fingers—not the thumb—get fingerpads. (The kit comes with six fingerpads, but you only need four at one time.)

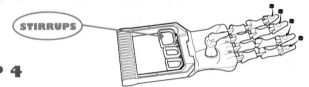

STIRRUPS

STEP 4

To use your Skeletal Hand, hold the grip and insert your fingers into the stirrups. (Notice that your pinkie and ring finger fit into the same large stirrup.) Pull on the stirrups to move the Skeletal Hand's fingers.

For a creepy skeleton effect, pull your sleeve over your real hand and the grip!